Solving the Pi

For Spiritual Seekers

By Prashant S. Shah

Available from Amazon and Kindle bookstore

ISBN-13: 978-1518786655

ISBN-10: 1518786650

ASIN: B0176HQSOG

Address: H-901 Nilamber Bellissimo, Vasna-Bhayli Road, Vadodara 391 410, Gujarat, India.

Email: prashantshah@alum.mit.edu

Site on Internet at http://spiritual-living.in

Contents

PREFACE

By the Author

Do you have a life problem?
Does the problem persist?
Do you feel that you are not going to find
the solution easily?

GOOD! Keep this problem before you and then begin to read this book. The problem will lead you on. As you go through these pages you will discover many wonderful things about life.

However, you may ask: *"Will it solve my problem?"* Well, it will clear up many things for you; but it will also open up newer issues. The problems of life are not there merely to be solved. They are there to lead you into the adventure of life. So, maybe you should try to enjoy the problem-solving process instead of rushing to reach the solution.

The ships are safe in the harbour. But that is not what ships are made for. They are there so that we can sail through the rough seas and visit distant lands. It is the same with the problems of our life. We can endure our problems and seek to avoid them; or we can treat them as opportunities to grow and enjoy the process of problem-solving. *What will it be?*

When we think spiritually, we consider that the people who are involved with us and the happenings of our life are given to us. They provide us the opportunities that we need to grow. Just as a car needs the ground to move forward, a bird needs the air to fly, we need the resistance from life (the problems) to grow and mature.

This book will take you on a problem-solving journey. The journey passes through three chapters. First, you learn to develop the right attitude towards your problems and life situations. Next, you go further and learn what you can do to experience freedom and contentment in your life. And lastly, you learn to gain control over your attention and use it to overcome the problems created by your personal thoughts and emotions.

Some Opinions Received:

1. 'Solving the Problems of Life' is a gem of a book. It has short chapters each of which has a depth well beyond its length. Each chapter can be read over and over again, discovering new meaning with each reading. The writing is clear and precise but the book must be read slowly so as to understand its myriad meanings. The emphasis on mantra is unusual and stimulating. At first, it seems impossible that such a simple process would have such deep effects, but practice proves its truth. I recommend this book very highly to readers who are serious about deepening their spiritual being... **Renana Jhabwala, New Delhi**

2. I liked the chapter on Mantra Yoga. The way the concept has been explained and carried through from 'what happens', 'why that happens', to the practical considerations, expectations, etc. makes the reading journey very engaging. The book spoke a lot to me and

it was a very good experience going through it... **Saket Vaidya, Pune**.

3. The book put me into a deep spiritual mood; and the mood grew on me as I continued to read... Here the root causes of our problems are explained in a very simple way. The ideas are truly thought provoking and the insight is really very good... **Sanjeev Vaidya, Chhindwara**.

4. Your earlier booklet on the subject was very inspiring and useful. But this new and expanded version of the book is simply superb. It is very readable and very satisfying, and I just couldn't stop reading it. The situations in life often make me lose my way, but this book has again got me thinking straight. I've decided to trust life, to accept the events as they come, and to focus on learning what life is teaching me... **Carmen Ambert, Puerto Rico**

5. The key message here is to take a spiritual approach to life. The book not only helps us in solving the problems of our life, but it also changes our entire outlook to life. I recommend it to all those who want to live a truly joyful, meaningful, and peaceful life... *Dr. V. W. Poflee, Nagpur.*

6. This is a book by a yogi who has disguised himself as an ordinary person! The writing is crystal clear and the articulation is very lucid and brilliant. It gives a very deep insight into the issues of life. The author has liberally shared some of his personal-life experiences to inspire the readers. Whereas the book is easy to read, it requires some re-reading to grasp the ideas... *J. V. Joshi, Baroda.*

7. This book shows how you can develop your connection with a higher consciousness. The writing is concise and yet sufficiently descriptive. It provides a deep understanding of human nature; how to face up to your

challenges, how to overcome your negative thoughts and emotions, and how to harness the power of your concentration and will using the mantra. I strongly recommend the book...
Marcus Ubl, London.

Chapter-1

SOLVING PROBLEMS THROUGH UNDERSTANDING

1. Understand the trials of life

Trials in life come, only to go away. While they stay, they challenge us. In meeting their challenge, we develop our potential — we develop the powers, abilities and capacities that are potential within us.

Just as a rough sea will develop an excellent captain, difficult times produce great human beings. Hence, whenever you are in difficulty, choose to accept the challenge. Then the strength to meet the situation will emerge from within you.

Try to remain calm and the force of the disturbance will weaken. Look for solutions, and you will discover newer and better ways to deal with the difficulty. Then persist in applying the solutions and something will surely work out for you.

2. Lessen the suffering

When there is no escape from pain or suffering, try to lessen the pain. Use the following suggestions:

a) *Become absorbed* in doing something that really interests you: Read a book by your favourite author, play a game that you enjoy, or engage in any activity that gives you joy. When you shift your attention from the pain it will become less.

b) Don't pray to escape from the suffering, but call for the *strength to endure* it and to come out better from experiencing it. That prayer will certainly be rewarded.

c) Think that the suffering will enlarge your awareness or *enrich your experience* in some way. Hence, you will come out better after suffering. Allow this thought to settle in your mind. It will cheer you up.

d) Think that your pain is *cancelling some old debt* that you had incurred – due to some wrong thought or action that you had done in the past. Feel happy to be released from the debt.

e) Believe that *you are much more* and other than the suffering that you are experiencing right now. The suffering is only in an external part of you. Hence, it is not of any great consequence, and it will also pass away in time.

f) The feeling of suffering arises in you since you have become attached to some things. As a spiritual being you can suffer *only when you are attached to something below*. Hence, try to lessen the attachment. Then your suffering will also become less. Further, know that you are not fated to suffer for nothing; and one day you will also experience happiness and freedom of your spiritual being.

3. Find guidance

When you are puzzled by a difficulty, you have to seek guidance:

a) Seek the advice of a *kind and wise person*. His sincere and sympathetic advice will provide a new light to you. It will greatly help you in resolving your doubt, difficulty or problem.

b) If you cannot find such a person, read a *book of sayings* or writings of some wise person. A passage here and there will strike you and give you the necessary clue.

c) If you are unable to have the assistance of such a person or book, then sit quietly by yourself with eyes closed and try to get in touch with the *guiding intelligence* that lies deeper within you. Don't keep on thinking about the problem or its solution. Just point out the problem and *ask* the unseen intelligence to help you and point out the way. At some time later on you will receive a new idea or a suggestion.

4. Use understanding

You can clear up many of your problems and difficulties with mere understanding. Consider the following:

a) Our world is under a higher authority, which is always balanced and just. Hence, all your actions have their consequence. However, the consequences do not arise immediately. There is a *time lag*. This time lag deceives people into thinking that there is no justice.

However, there is a proper time, a proper place and a natural sequence for everything that happens. What is happening now has in it the consequence of what has been done in the past. What happens in future will also bear the consequence of what you are doing -just now. Thus, if you want to make a better future, you have to use your time and energy to do the right things now.

b) Consider your *difficulties as tests* that are given to prepare you for greater tasks. They will develop your skills and capacity. Hence, your difficulties will develop the power that you need to overcome the weakness within you and outside you.

c) Everything that happens in the world serves some purpose. Then, after the purpose is served, it goes away. Hence, your *difficulty will also pass away*. However, while the difficulty is there, recognise why it has come. Ask yourself: Have you been unjust? Are you neglecting something important? Be quick to recognise your fault and correct it. Then your difficulty will also pass away.

d) Consider your difficulty as something that has arisen in an *external part of you*. When you think like that, the difficulty will not be able to unsettle you. Then it will be easier for you to find a clue to the solution.

e) People experience the thoughts they think. Hence, you must *be careful about what you keep on thinking*. When you think sad thoughts, you become sad. When you think happy thoughts, you become cheerful. Hence, choose to dwell on thoughts of courage, kindness, love and fellowship. Don't think of the painful memories from the past.

f) There is a *blessing in every difficulty* or change. In the hopes that have been frustrated; in the ageing of the body; in the troubles and trials of life; and in the works that have not yet succeeded there is a blessing. Hence, when you experience a difficulty, think of the good that has come out of it or can come out of it. Allow that thought to add the element of enthusiasm and joy to your life.

5. Consider yourself as something special

Your existence as a human being is something special. A spiritual world is awaiting the opportunity to find its expression through you. The consciousness of the Supreme Being dwells inside you. Hence, never condemn yourself. Listen to the quiet voice of your conscience and allow it to guide your affairs.

As a person you are *unique*. No two human beings are exactly alike. Your experience, your nature, your origin, your life situation, and the purpose you are serving are all unique. You are connected with others in such a way that there is something that only you can fulfil. In this world there is something that only you can do. Hence, do what you have to do with enthusiasm and feel supported by God.

Nature is beautiful, but it cannot give a smile like you. The city has beautiful constructions, but they cannot tell a story as you can. The Sun rises punctually to do its duty, but it cannot sympathize with others like you can. It cannot be a little less hot in the summer and a little warmer in the winter. The flowing waters can give you a soothing feeling, but they cannot comfort others like you can. Birds can fly freely in the sky, but they do not find the fulfilment that comes with the human toil.

6. Be optimistic

When you are optimistic you can find an opportunity in every difficulty. You can be hopeful, confident and make the best use of the circumstances of your life.

When you are pessimistic you see difficulties in every opportunity. You believe that people are bad and everything is becoming worse. Thus, you anticipate and invite frustration and sorrow in your life.

Optimism always softens the blow: The accident is not as bad as you had feared; the hill is not as steep as you thought before you started to climb; the difficulty is not as great as you had anticipated; and everything will turn out much better than you had expected. Pessimism, on the other hand, always deepens the blow. It exaggerates the trouble and makes the difficulty harder to overcome.

Hence, optimism is a heavenly quality. You have not come here on earth to suffer or be wasted. Something great and wonderful is being worked out in you and through you. So,

be optimistic and try to fulfil what you have
come to do.

7. Be wise

There are many 'unseen persons' that act through you. When you are aware of these persons, you can *choose* which person will decide your behaviour. Let us consider four kinds of persons: the wise, the intelligent, the ordinary and the foolish.

The *wise* person looks for the feedback on his actions. He quickly becomes aware of his mistake and quietly tries to correct it.

The *intelligent* person only recognises his mistake when it shows up. However, he accepts the mistake and prepares to correct it.

The *ordinary* person is unable to recognize his own mistake. If someone points out his mistake he argues with him and tries to justify his action.

The *foolish* person becomes furious if someone points out his fault. He is unwilling to see his personal contribution to the problem. Instead, he blames others or the circumstances for his difficulties. For some things to improve in his life, he demands that first the other people or the circumstances should change. Thus, his mistakes continue and his problems repeat.

8. Do not create problems for yourself

The world we live in is relative. The opposites and contrary views co-exist in the world. Thus, what you like, some others may dislike. What you denounce, some others may admire. What you treasure, some others may consider as worthless. What others seek and pursue, you may be trying to get rid of.

You have a reason for your view, but others also have reasons for their views. So, respect others for what they are and try to *accommodate* their views. You have to accept that there cannot be just one right view when there are so many different interests in the world.

When you meet people who are rigid in their views and ways, don't try to change them. They aren't sufficiently ready to improve or change. Hence, don't argue with them or clash with them. Be intelligent and learn to *move around* these rigid rocks. Then you will not create unnecessary problems for yourself.

9. Overcome your inner enemies

The inner and outer aspects of your life are related. You meet your inner enemies in the people and situations of your life. The weakness in your nature shows up in the difficulties that you experience. Hence, if some of your difficulties are repeating, ask: "*Why is this happening to me*". Recognize the inner weakness which is the cause and then seek to overcome it.

Your habits and tendencies are the creations of your past. They arise out of how you have thought and acted in the past. These habits decide your subconscious cravings and inclinations today. To be able to choose correctly in any situation, first you have to become free from these inner compulsions.

Your habits and tendencies will change as you change the motives with which you act. You can begin the change by disallowing your personal and selfish thoughts to motivate your thinking. Instead, *allow your actions to be guided by the sense of dharma.* Do only what you think is kind or proper.

Keep up this practice for a few years and you will be blessed with a lot of good luck.

10. Seek counsel

If you are struggling in some aspect of your life, or if some difficulties are repeating, you need the help of someone who can see from *outside* of your frame of reference.

A wise counsellor will look differently at your difficulty. Such a person can clarify your ideas, evaluate your options and give you a clue to the causes. To uproot the problem you have to remove the cause and not merely relieve the effects. You have to find the right things to do and do them properly.

However, to receive good counsel you have to be open and flexible: You have to be *willing* to regard things differently; you must believe that your problem is solvable and that you are partly responsible for it; and that the outcome of what happens in the future will depend to an extent on what you do now.

11. Don't ask for blessings, count your blessings

If you ask for blessings and you don't get what you want, you get frustrated. Then you become sceptical and a non-believer in God. However, if you carefully review the happenings of your life, you will notice the numerous occasions on which you got help without having to ask. These are your blessings. Count them.

Counting your blessings will develop your trust in the unseen guide and companion of your life. This inner being is there. It has always been there watching over you from behind a veil. And it is waiting for you to internalize your mind to unveil it.

When you find this inner being, you have found the true treasure of life. All the things you have today are in the realm of death. They are there only for a while; and one day you will have to leave them behind. But the inner being, the guide and companion of your life, will never forsake you.

12. *The School of Life*

When you take up a physical body, you have
taken your admission into the school of life.
You have come to earth with a certain amount
of energy and aptitudes, and in this school you
are given some lesson to learn. You learn
through a process of trial and error. Thus, your
failures are a part of the process that will lead
to your growth and maturing.

In the school of life you *cannot avoid* learning
the lesson that you are given. If you try to do
that your difficulties and trials will keep on
repeating. They will repeat in some form or the
other until you have learnt your lesson. Further,
you will be given the next lesson of the higher
class only *after* you have matured through the
lessons that have already been given to you.

When you have learnt your lesson, you have
passed the exam of your class in the school of
life. Then you will get the lesson of the next
class. There is no part of your life that does not
have a lesson for you. The process of learning

through lessons does not end. So, if you are alive, there is still something you have to learn!

Sometimes you want to learn a *different lesson* from the one that life is teaching you right now. However, you do not get this opportunity until life presents it to you. Hence, you should confine your attention to learn the lesson that life is teaching you right now.

The people that you connect up with on earth are a *part of the drama* of your life. Thus, your enemies and friends are also given to you. They provide the obstacles and opportunities in your learning process. The aptitudes and resources that you have right now are also related to the lesson that is set for you to learn.

The education in the school of life, however, is informal. Hence, you are given the lesson, but how you perform will always be up to you. You can use the opportunity to grow or you can waste it. You can learn fast, go slow or postpone learning. Thus, you can learn a lot or very little. How well you do in the school of life will depend on how intelligently you *conduct* yourself.

Chapter-2:

FREEDOM & CONTENTMENT
AND HOW TO EXPERIENCE THEM

The spiritual tradition in ancient India talks in terms of karma and dharma. When you act with personal or selfish motives you generate some imbalance, which is called karma. When you do what is proper and act without personal motives you generate balance and harmony, which is called dharma. Freedom and contentment are built on the foundation of Dharma.

In society the acts of dharma are *fairness* in dealings; *balance* in rights and obligations; *restricting* individual freedom where it transgresses the freedom of other people; *subordinating* personal benefit for the benefit of the team, group or unity; and *serving* the genuine needs of others.

True freedom and contentment are inner-life attainments. And to experience them you have to make some adjustments in your attitude and assumptions according to the rules of dharma or proper living. *What are these changes and how can you make them?*

1. Make the necessary inner changes

The ancient sages believed that there is a pre-decided element regarding all the major events of our life. The events are outcomes of past actions; other players are involved with the events; and there are hidden intelligences in the interior worlds that have their own agenda. Hence, it is said that *we arrive at the events* of our life. Our efforts in the present only make some cosmetic changes or adjustments.

So, whether we like it or not we have to accept the happenings of our life. We can do it in the same way as we accept other things that we cannot control – like the weather, the past, the market behaviour, etc. When we can do that, we can live peacefully and without experiencing frustration. On the other hand, if we keep on protesting or defying the situations of our life, we only hurt ourselves.

Whereas we cannot control the events that are happening now or are decided for us, there are many things that we can control. For example, we can control our expectations and how we respond to other people and events. We can always choose how we interpret the happenings in the world. Hence, instead of crying over the things we cannot control, we have to focus on controlling the things we can control.

First let us distinguish between what is under our control and what is not under our control: Our actions are always under our control, but another person's actions are usually not under our control. We can influence other people's behaviour by how we relate with them (by how we regard them, take interest in them, etc.) but we can never control them sufficiently. We must accept this reality just as we accept the other things that we cannot control.

When we keep our focus on controlling the things that are under our control, our attention is automatically directed to our own actions. We become more aware of our attitude, beliefs and actions; and the effect they have on other people and the happenings in our life. When we can observe all this, we become intensely aware of the inner changes that we need to make to be able to live a more peaceful and contented life.

You begin by becoming clear about what changes are under your control and what changes are not under your control. Then you accept the things you cannot change, and focus on making the changes you really need to make.

Here we explain the rules of dharma so that you can know the changes that you need to make.

2. Freedom and how to achieve it

Is freedom doing whatever we please, or does our freedom arise from understanding the limits of our power and the limits set by society, the natural law, and a higher authority?

To appreciate the idea of freedom first we have to understand how our wants control our actions: When we want something desperately, we get totally focused on having it irrespective of whether it is good for us, appropriate for us, or morally right for us. The only thing we see is the object that satisfies our want. We disregard other things or undervalue them. In this way our wants control our actions.

To experience freedom first we have to weaken our bondage (slavery) to our wants – to the cravings and compulsions that arise from within our nature. To do that, we have to deliberately regulate our wants. We have to give due regard to what is proper for us in society (according to the moral law) and what is enough (according to the natural law). We have to accept our limitations and the inevitable; and learn to work with them rather than try to fight them.

If we become easily obsessed by the desire to do things that are not right for us or which are not within our reach, our freedom is actually lost! If we cannot exercise control over our wants, the desires in our mind and body will enslave us. Then we cannot perform the duty of our roles properly. Then our actions will become out of sorts and we shall experience helplessness and frustration!

Thus, true freedom is not having ease and comfort; it is not bossing over others; and it is not doing whatever comes into our mind regardless of others. To experience true freedom you have to be able to conduct yourself according to the existing situation *without* giving in to your personal tendencies or temptations. It demands that you accept the limits of your power and the limits that are set on you by a greater authority.

3. Approach life as a banquet

Sometimes we think that if we don't grab our share in life we shall miss out; if we don't horde our wealth we shall get depleted. We think like this when we feel insecure; it causes us to grab things.

However, as a human being we are a part of a larger network that is governed by a greater intelligence and authority. We are connected to others on the inner planes; there is a law governing human life; and there is a greater intelligence in the inner worlds that administers justice and looks over our affairs. As a result we are only given things according to the needs of our roles or according to what we have deserved (according to the law of karma).

So, when we take the roles that we are given, we have to also trust that the greater authority will provide us with what we need to fulfil our roles. It will not make us struggle unnecessarily. When we understand this fact we can behave graciously in all situations. We know that we shall be given a part to play in the drama of life on earth; and that we shall be provided with what we need to fulfil that role or part.

When we understand this, we can approach our life as a BANQUET: When dishes are passed on to us, we take a moderate portion. If a dish passes us, we enjoy what is already on our plate. Or, if the dish hasn't been passed on to us yet, we wait patiently for our turn to arrive.

When we choose to act according to dharma, we can never become jealous of others. When we find that someone has succeeded, we consider that today it is their time to succeed. Our time will also come. However, if we become impatient and grab for things before it is their time to arrive, we spoil everything.

The rule is: Always behave graciously in life and keep an attitude of polite restraint. Trust that what is due to you will come to you in the natural course, when your time has come.

4. Act well the part that is given to you

We get to choose only some of our roles life. Most of the roles that we have are given to us.

We are like actors in a play. A greater authority has assigned us with some roles without consulting us! Some people will act in a short drama, and others will act in a big movie. Some are assigned the part of a poor or retarded person and some are given the role of a celebrity or a leader.

Although we cannot control which roles are assigned to us, we are always responsible to act our given roles as best as we can, and to refrain from protesting them.

This brings us to the classical issue of dharma: *Should we crave for different or better roles or should we seek to perform well in the roles that are given to us? Does our true satisfaction arise from getting into positions of great opportunity or does it arise from how well we perform in the roles we are given?*

To choose here we have to see things in the correct perspective. We must understand that our true happiness does not arise from the roles themselves. It arises from within us as we perform the roles.

Thus, true fulfilment arises when we perform well in the roles that we are given. The outer conditions only provide us with the situations in life. However, it is up to us to make ourselves happy or sad as we pass through these situations.

Thus, it is a deception to think that our happiness arises from getting better or more attractive roles. Further, if we keep on craving for better roles in life, we shall remain continuously dissatisfied.

Hence, seek to perform the roles that you are given as best as you can – without protesting your situation. In whatever circumstances you find yourself, give an impeccable performance. If you are a teacher, teach well; if you are a maid, serve well; and if you are leader, lead well.

5. All advantages have their price

Does somebody enjoy the privileges, the opportunities, or the honour that you desire? Does it make you feel jealous, envious, inferior, or unfortunate?

We become jealous of others when we think that they got it easier or they did not deserve what they got. However, this is a deception. It arises because we have a partial or limited view of things.

When we take a wider view of things, we can see that people get authority and resources according to the needs of their roles or they get it according to their karma. The law of justice has no favourites — it works invariably for all.

If we look at situations carefully, we can find advantages and disadvantages in every situation. Hence, no situation is absolutely more favourable or unfavourable. Further, authority is not merely a privilege. Authority and responsibility always go together. They are like the two ends of the same stick. When we pick up one end, we also get the other.

Still further, our happiness also does not really depend on the situation we are in. It depends more on what we make out of the situation that we are in. We can never earn the same reward as others without employing similar methods, or without investing a similar amount of time and effort. It is unreasonable to think that we can have the rewards without paying the price.

Hence, we should not envy those who have more than us. They had no real advantage over us. They have simply paid the price for their reward.

The true reward that people get in real life can also be very deceptive. The saying is, *"The roses come with the thorns"*; but the thorns are not always apparent to a superficial view. A man may have a beautiful wife, but she may crib all the time because she was used to having too much attention. An actress may have to show a happy face even when she inwardly feels degraded by what she is asked to do.

In our life it is always up to us to choose from the opportunities we get; and to decide how much we shall invest in it. For some things we may consider the price as too high: It may cost us our integrity; we may be forced to praise or appease someone whom we cannot respect; we may have to do the work for which we are not apt; or we may have to convince the people of things that we ourselves don't believe in!

The truth is that all privileges have their price. So, before you demand something, ask the golden question: *What is the price and are you willing to pay it?*

6. Our duties are revealed by our relationships

In society we are not an isolated entity, but a unique and irreplaceable part of a network in a perfectly ordered human community. Hence, *it is important to know where we fit into this web or network.*

Our duties in society are defined by our relation with others. To know our duties we have to look carefully at the people we are connected with. Our duties emerge naturally from our family, our neighbourhood, our workplace, our community or our nation. Our role as a parent, a child, a wife, a neighbour, a manager, a citizen, etc. arises from our duty. Once we know our role to the people we are linked with, we can intuitively know what are the right things to do.

For example, if a person is our father, certain emotional and practical claims follow from this relationship. There is a natural link between us, and accordingly, we are obliged to care for him in old age; to listen to his advice even when we think differently; and to regard him with respect.

However, let us suppose that he is not a good father — that he is uneducated, crude, or holds outdated views. Then we have to ask ourselves: *Does nature give everyone an ideal father, or just a father?* When it comes to our duty as a son or daughter, whatever our father's nature may be, whatever his personal habits are is secondary. The greater authority has not designed people or circumstance according to our tastes. Whether we find this person to be agreeable or not, he is still our father, and so it is our duty to live up to our obligations.

Suppose we have a brother or sister who treats us badly. *Why should that make a difference?* We still have a moral obligation to recognise and maintain our fundamental duty to him or her. The key to dharma is not focus on what he or she does, but simply look to ourselves and try to serve the role the greater authority has assigned to us – and to do it to the best of our ability.

True and authentic freedom places demands on you. It requires that you accept the obligations of your role and perform your duties sincerely. So, let others behave as they will; that is not within your control anyway, and so it should not concern you very much. The only question that should concern you is: *"What is your duty and are you serving it?"*

7. Control your interpretations

When we carry out our actions according to our duty, the greater intelligence or authority will support us. Then, we shall not feel victimised by the words or deeds of others. If others are selfish or ungrateful, we should take it that they are performing their duty poorly. *Why should we let that bother us?*

Except for extreme physical abuse, other people cannot hurt us unless we allow them to. If we don't consent to be hurt, we won't be hurt. Whatever happens in the world outside, it is always up to us to choose how we interpret it. So, our interpretation of events is a choice over which we can have absolute control!

People think of events or people as being good or bad, but we can ask: *"What is a good event?"* or *"What is a bad event?"* There is really no such thing. If there is a fire in our enemy's camp, we may call it a good event. If there is a fire in our camp, we may call it a bad event. Otherwise the event by itself is value neutral. It simply happens. In the same way, there are really no 'good people' or 'bad people' out there. Each person has come to earth with his or her purpose. For some time destiny brings some people together. Then we find some people to be agreeable and some to be disagreeable.

Hence the rule is: Never react to events. Instead, *exercise control over your interpretation of the events.* When you can exercise that control, the events cannot hurt you or make you feel sad

8. Serve the greater purpose

When we consider the future, we must understand that all situations and events unfold as they do regardless of how we feel about them. Our hopes and fears sway us, but not the events!

Hence, a wise person does not project his hopes and fears onto the future. Such projections can only generate fantasies. There is a place for planning and making provision for uncertainties. But true preparation for life consists in developing self-control and good personal habits. And to make this preparation, we have to review our actions from time to time so that we can keep them free from the hold of fear, greed, jealousy or neglect.

Do not allow the happenings in your life to distract you from serving your greater purpose. To serve the greater purpose, just keep one question in your mind: *"What is the proper thing for me to do right now and how can I get on to doing it?"*

Summary

True freedom and contentment are inner-life attainments, and to experience them you have to make some adjustments in your attitude and assumptions according to the rules of dharma or proper living. *Here is a summary of the changes that you need to make:*

- You begin by becoming clear about what changes are under your control and what changes are not under your control. Then you accept the things you cannot change, and focus on making the changes you really need to make.
- True freedom is not having ease and comfort; it is not bossing over others; and it is not doing whatever comes into our mind regardless of others. To experience true freedom you have to be able to conduct yourself according to the existing situation *without* giving in to your personal tendencies or temptations. You have to accept the limits of your power and the

limits that are set on you by a greater authority.

- Always behave graciously in life and keep an attitude of polite restraint. Trust that what is due to you will come to you in the natural course, when your time has come.

- Seek to perform the roles that you are given as best as you can – without protesting your situation. In whatever circumstances you find yourself, *give an impeccable performance*.

- All privileges have their price. So, before you demand something, ask the golden question: *What is the price and are you willing to pay it?*

- True and authentic freedom requires that you accept the obligations of your role and perform your duties sincerely. So, let others behave as they will; that is not within your control anyway, and so it should not concern you very much. The only question that should concern you is: *"What is your duty and are you serving it?"*

- Never react to events. Instead, exercise *control over your interpretation* of the events. When you can exercise that control, the events cannot hurt you or make you feel sad.
- To serve the greater purpose in your life, just keep one question in your mind: *"What is the proper thing for me to do right now and how can I get on to doing it?"*

When you make the above said changes in your belief system, you will be guided by a greater intelligence. Then you can experience freedom and contentment in your life. Then the feeling of helplessness and frustration will become a thing of the past.

Chapter-3:

THE MARVEL OF MANTRA YOGA

a) Spiritual Yoga

Yoga has been introduced in the western world as a technique for reducing stress and improving health. However, the traditional purpose of Yoga is to develop the spiritual life.

Here we explore this 'spiritual side' of Yoga.
The term Yoga is a common noun that means
'uniting'. It is the practice of joining or *attuning*
the personal consciousness, our mind, with the
universal consciousness, which can be referred
to as a higher consciousness, God or the soul. It
is concerned with developing the 'subject-side'
of our existence and not the object or material
side.

1 What happens in Yoga?

Yoga increases our awareness of the higher
consciousness and detaches it from the
ordinary consciousness, which is from our
personal memories, desires and possessions. In
Yoga we achieve the higher consciousness by
persistently dwelling or meditating on an image
of it. Then spiritual qualities begin to arise in
our mind, and it becomes easier for us to
overcome the personal tendency that keeps
our awareness bound to our animal nature.
Gradually our awareness expands and we begin
to see everything from a more interior part of

our being. Then we see the larger picture; we develop a deeper insight into the issues of life; and we take a more inclusive point of view in social matters.

Why does that happen? Although externally all human beings are like parts of the cosmos; internally they are 'microcosms' or lesser wholes. The human being can be compared to a small slice of the big cosmic cake. The slice contains all the ingredients of the cake. In the same way, all the powers and intelligences that exist in the external cosmos also exist in some form within the human constitution. And God, the Lord of the cosmos, is also our ultimate being.

Our existence as a human being can be compared to the *life of a leaf on a tree*. As long as a leaf feels itself as 'separate' from the tree, it will fear the fall season, when it has to dry up and wither away. However, the ultimate consciousness of the leaf is also the consciousness of the tree. Hence, if the leaf can break the bonds that separate it in consciousness from the tree, then it can also experience the larger consciousness of the tree. Then it will lose its fear of death and look upon the fall season merely as a renewal.

In the same way, as our inner life grows we begin to experience the higher levels of consciousness in the cosmos. It changes our outlook, our insight and our understanding of life. As a result we experience a change of mind and a change of heart. We become more aware and more considerate.

2. How do you begin?

You normally begin by gaining control over your attention. When you have sufficient control, you can change many things in your life: You can re-organise your priorities; you can concentrate on your tasks without distraction; and your decisions are not easily influenced by your personal desires and preferences.

Further, once you can control your attention, you can use it to clear the negative thoughts and negative emotions from your mind. That is important, since you experience the thoughts and emotions that occupy your mind. Your mental state, that is your happiness and well-being, depends more on how you handle the thoughts and emotions and less on your external circumstances. Hence, you don't have to be successful to become happy. You can remain joyful even when things are going bad.

In this introduction you learn three things: First, you observe the drifting tendency of the mind. Next, you learn how to control your attention. And then you learn how you can bring a higher consciousness into your life.

3. Observing the mind — an illustration

First, let us observe the restless and the emotional nature of our mind and notice the presence of our will inside it. The *task*: Sit comfortably in a chair with eyes closed and think of an object, such as a "MANGO". Keep the attention on thoughts relating to the mango. Every time you notice that the attention has drifted away from the theme, you mark a cross on a paper and return your attention to the mango. Do the exercise for three minutes and notice the number of crosses you have marked. Do this again after practicing the 'returning exercise' for a month and you will find that the number of crosses will reduce.

Let me tell you what happened when I did this exercise: My attention began to **drift**. Many thoughts began to flow into my mind. At first, I saw the orange colour of the mango. Next, I noticed that my mind has jumped onto a thought about my dyestuffs factory, which manufactures yellow colour. From there, my mind did not return to a thought relating to the mango. Instead, I began to worry about the labour problems in my factory!

In another sequence of dwelling on the mango-image I began to think of the fruit market. The next thought told me that fruits are becoming expensive these days. From there my mind did not return onto the thoughts relating to the mango. It strayed onto a thought of the prices on the stock exchange; I began to fear a fall in the prices.

My observation: In every sequence, something inside my mind kept on pulling at my chain of thought. Hence, I could not sufficiently dwell on my chosen theme. My attention drifted from the chosen theme to *associated* thoughts and from there to thoughts that were totally *unrelated* to my chosen subject.

4. Overcoming the drifting tendency

In yoga, you overcome this tendency by subjecting your mind to a steady pressure of your will. *What happens?* It gradually brings all the forces that scatter or divide your attention UNDER the control of your will.

Then you can concentrate on a task even if it is *not appealing*. Your mind will not generate aversions. When there is a *difficulty*, your mind will not generate a reaction or create a panic. It will remain calm and objective and allow you to think clearly and act appropriately.

Thus, by overcoming the drifting tendency of the mind, you develop *self-control*. It is not some external control by someone else. It is your control over the forces that are inside your mind. When you have this control, your mind will be your greatest asset. It will allow you to remain inwardly calm and peaceful during difficult times; and outwardly you can get more focused on performing your tasks. With this combination, you will do much better in all your undertakings.

5. What exactly is concentration?

When you concentrate something, you bring some things 'together'. It increases their strength. In chemistry, you remove the solvent to make a substance more concentrated. An example of concentration in physics is to bundle a bunch of sticks together. It is easy to break one stick at a time. However, when they are bundled together, it increases their strength. Then you cannot break them easily. For the same reasons people tend to concentrate in society to form groups and communities. It increases their strength and as a group they become a force to reckon with. Then, as a group, they can make a better impact against the resistance in their environment.

What concentration does in spiritual practice: It brings together all the scattered forces of your attention. It is like bringing the different chieftains under a 'central leadership'. Gradually all the forces inside the mind begin to acknowledge the presence of your will. Then they adjust themselves under the dictates of your will. As a result it will be easier for you to concentrate your attention and overcome the internal divisions and the contradictory forces inside your mind. Then your mind will become *one-pointed or sharp.*

6. The practice

In India there are many village festivals in which a celebrated person comes in riding on an elephant. If the elephant is idle, he picks up little things from the shops or street and tosses them around. However, if his attention is kept occupied, like when he is holding an umbrella to give shelter to the person in front, he does not do any mischief. Our mind is also like this elephant. First, you have to give the mind a theme to hold on to. Then, you can put a steady pressure of your will on it and confine your attention to that theme.

The theme that you use for the concentration practice is called the seed (bija) for meditation.

The common seeds that are used are as follows: You turn over the beads of a rosary (mala); you gaze at a diagram (yantra) or light (flame); you listen to the internal vibration of a mantra; or you sense the act of breathing. In every case the practice is to confine your attention to the seed or theme. You have to only persist with the practice and your mind will settle down and get concentrated.

The natural tendency of the mind is to drift onto other thoughts, particularly to thoughts of pending matters and personal concerns. So, your attention will stray onto other thoughts. However, when you find that your attention has strayed, your task is to simply return it to your chosen theme or the seed of meditation.

*The act of **persistently returning** your attention to the chosen theme makes all the difference*: Gradually all the forces inside the mind begin to acknowledge the presence of your will. Then they adjust themselves and accept your leadership. It is similar to what happens when a shepherd waves his staff at the sheep. The sheep accept the directive and fall in line or join the flock. This is what happens as your mind gets concentrated.

7. On Mantra Yoga

All spiritual techniques have their advantages, but the technique of Mantra Yoga has some special advantages. Here you nurture a spiritual vibration within your system that has a leading quality. It *alters* the personal vibration that you carry in your mindset. And that inclines you to think differently and respond to the happenings in life differently.

Thus, the mantra practice will gradually change your attitude; it will change how you regard everything (what arguments you buy into); and it will change where (in what places) you look for your satisfaction. Then you begin to connect up with different kind of people; you eat different kind of food; you value things differently; and you act with different motives.

Further, the mantra maintains your connection with a spiritual influence, and that greatly simplifies your spiritual practice. Then you don't have to search blindly for directions in your life. You can know the right thing to do intuitively by mirroring the higher consciousness. Then your spiritual task is to simply overcome the resistance generated in your mind.

8. The key idea of Yoga

Wisdom and the higher values arise naturally in your mind when you involve a higher consciousness in your life. Hence, to grow spiritually you do not have to develop the ordinary human consciousness, the mind, through an intellectual process. Instead, you have to discipline the mind and make it more *receptive* to the higher consciousness!

When the higher consciousness becomes active in your life, it will directly speak in your mind. Then you can know the truth in matters of life through an internal process. Then you will not be easily deceived by the illusions that are generated by contents (the desires and tendencies) of your mind.

9. Is Spiritual Yoga theistic or atheistic?

Let us consider the two different points of view. The atheistic view regards God as an imaginary concept or a belief. On the other hand the theistic view regards God as a spiritual presence that you can learn to perceive and relate with.

Spiritual Yoga is essentially a theistic pursuit. It uses a personal (self-made) God to deliberately bring about a *shift* in the focus of your life – from the ordinary consciousness to the higher consciousness. As the focus changes, it also changes your experience of yourself and the world. Then, instead of perceiving yourself to be a personality that arises out of a mind and body, now you begin to regard yourself as a spiritual being that is temporarily functioning on earth through the instruments of a mind and body. It will open up the truly mystical dimension of your life.

b) Using Mantra Yoga

1. My introduction to a mantra

This was my first spiritual lesson. I'll narrate how I got the mantra and what it did for me. Then I'll show you how you can practice concentration effectively by simply chanting a mantra.

I had a difficult childhood. It was due to an *'attention deficiency'* – my mind used to wander about and so I could not dwell on any theme for a long time. I would either get restless or become impatient. As a result, I was very weak in studies. Let me narrate an incident that happened after I had completed the final exam in the fifth standard.

I visited the school with my elder brother for a 'cubs' (junior scouts) meeting. After the meeting my brother wanted to visit the teacher's room to know how well he had done in the exams. We went to the teacher's room together, but he went in alone and I waited outside. After a few minutes my brother returned and announced that he had achieved the third rank in his class. That was very good. Unfortunately for me my teacher saw me waiting outside. So, she called out to me saying, *"Hey you there; please come in"*. I ignored the request as though I had not heard it. However, the teacher persisted and so I had to go in; and here is what happened:

I said, "Are you really calling me?"

She said, "Don't you want to know how well you have done in the exam?"

I replied, "Not particularly".

But the teacher persisted and said, *"But I want you to know"*. And then she added, *"You passed"*.

My face lit up, and I was keen to run away and announce the good news to my brother who was waiting outside. However, the teacher didn't let me get away so easily. She said, *"Don't you want to know why you passed?"*

"I must have done well," I replied.

"Nonsense," she said: "I passed you just because I don't want you in my class again!"

That remark hurt like a stab in the heart. However, I made no show of it and quietly left the teacher's room. By this time I had passed through many such situations. Such experiences made me defensive and I also developed many self-esteem issues. To cut the long story short, I was ultimately asked to leave the school. Fortunately for me my father had some influence in society and so he got me admitted into a boarding school.

At the boarding school I started out as a better student. However, gradually the old conditions started to repeat and I began to trail behind. One day the sports coach came to me after a game. He handed the football to me and asked me to get it into the goal. I said that should be easy since there is no one in between. However, the coach remarked: *"Let's see if you can do it"*. I accepted the challenge and began to run towards the goal, kicking the ball along with my feet. When I was near the goal I took a shot, but the ball missed the goal! The coach saw my sorry condition and offered to help. He asked me to visit him in the evening, after dinner.

In the evening he gave me a mantra and a small rosary (mala). He told me that I should chant the mantra along with turning over the beads – one recital per bead. I was to do the practice privately for fifteen minutes twice daily. He said: *"The chanting will please the goddess of learning and that will change everything for you"*. At that time, passing the final exam was most important for me. So I asked, *"Will it help me in passing my exam?"* And he replied, *"It will do that and much more. It will develop your ability to grasp ideas; it will build your character; and it will give you the inner support you need."* At the time I could not appreciate the other benefits, but the assurance that I would pass the exams was sufficient for me.

Where did this practice get me? Well, that year I just managed to pass the school exam. That was great. The next year I passed GCE 'O-level' (school leaving exam) in 3rd division (C grade). A year later I passed the first year exam in college with a 2nd division (B grade). And the next year I secured a 1st class (A grade) in the inter-science exam. My improvement continued and two years later I achieved admission into the famous MIT (Cambridge, Massachusetts) of USA as a transfer student. However, by then I had already achieved the good fortune of having a Guru, who totally changed the direction of my life.

2. My first benefits

Let me summarise what the mantra practice did for me:

1. Physically I became less restless or fidgety. The habit of rushing to do everything stopped.
2. Mentally, I became quiet. The self-talk that was continuously going on inside my mind became optional.
3. On the moral side, I simply stopped telling lies. I didn't want the humiliation that would come with getting caught. Hence, I started to believe that if I stand by the truth, the truth will also stand by me.
4. On the work side, I became more selective and focused. I took up fewer things to do and I took pride in doing them well.

Now I understood that the chanting practice not only concentrated the mind, but the quality of the mantra vibration also brought the mind under a spiritual influence. I was satisfied with the spiritual qualities and virtues that began to arise in my mind.

I am often asked: *"If it is so simple, why is everyone not using the mantra?"* Many people take up such practices, but most of them lack the discipline or the persistence. Hence, it does not lead to anything. For me the mantra was like a float that I saw in the sea of my life. I just held on to it tightly, and so it worked wonders for me.

3. The mantra tradition

What is the tradition of mantra practice? In priestly families in India the children are initiated at an early age into spiritual life with a mantra. The mantra that is given is the Gayatri mantra or a simple seed-mantra like Ram or Hrim. However, there are also some rules and disciplines that go along with the practice. They are as follows:

1.   You should take a mantra from someone who has attained some spiritual mastery through it. Through his or her presence you can easily find the inner connections that will get you on the spiritual path. (If you already have a personal mantra, please use it.)

2.   Chanting the mantra is not merely saying it. It is like an invocation. It is something that you utter with reverence and respect. Hence, it is not merely the technique or method that gets you the results, but the results are more a consequence of attuning your mind with the higher power. The higher

power grants. On your part you have to become ready and humble to receive.

3.   For the mantra to remain sacred, you have to keep it a personal secret. Hence, you should not reveal it to others. You can discuss the mantra practice in a general way, but you must not tell the actual mantra you are using. Let the people guess.

If you want an appropriate mantra from us, kindly write a little about yourself along with the commitment given below:

"I believe there is a spiritual being that is my caretaker. It is looking over my life and my existence. I want a mantra to establish my connection with it. I commit that I shall keep my mantra a secret."
Then send your application to us and we shall attend to it.

According to the Yoga tradition there is a spiritual being, like a guardian angel, behind every human being. It loves you dearly and knows you deeply. It knows your *past*: what you have been and what has made you what you are today. It also knows your *future*: it knows your secret desires and the conditions you will be passing through in your life. Hence, it can guide you correctly. The aim of the mantra practice is to open your mind to this influence.

Whatever reason you have today for starting your spiritual practice, as you progress it will change. The aim will be to live in communication with the higher consciousness.

4. The practice

The basic practice

Chant your mantra: Recite it slowly, in a rhythm of about one mantra per second. Do the chanting for fifteen minutes twice daily.

The traditional technique for chanting uses a *rosary* (mala) of about 30 small pea-sized wooden beads. You have to turn over one bead per recital. With a little practice the chanting will get into a rhythm.

The traditional method of *turning over* the beads is as follows: Bring together the tips of the ring finger and the thumb of the right hand to form a closed loop. Hold the rosary in the loop with the fingertips pointing downwards. Then turn over the beads with the third finger (middle finger), and not the index finger. Practice a few rounds and the chanting will become an enjoyable experience.

Once you get the recitation into a rhythm, the chanting will become like a 'muttering'. It will not be clearly audible, but it will release a pulse of energy with each recital.

Interruptions

Your chanting will get distracted by intruding thoughts. When you find that your attention has drifted onto some personal thought, don't get irritated. Simply resume the chanting.

Some practical considerations

Select a *time* and a *place* for doing the chanting exercise: The time should be such that you can keep to it regularly. The place should be a quiet and secluded corner of your house or room where you cannot be easily disturbed. In addition it will be helpful to have a *clock* that is visible, so that you do not have to wonder about the time.

The golden rule that I followed for doing the practice regularly was to put a *penalty* for missing any chanting session. I would miss the next meal.

Expectations

The benefits of chanting arise as you get involved with the practice. However, you may have to wait for some time before you can become aware of some significant changes within your nature. During this time you have to continue the practice with minimum expectations. Otherwise you spoil the practice.

Meditation
After you are comfortable with chanting the mantra, do the chanting for only ten minutes. Then stop chanting and allow the mantra to go on mentally. When you can do that comfortably, just sit quietly with the vibration. Then, go further and try to experience (perceive) the presence of your guiding spirit. Try to feel it. If you cannot experience it, still think that it is there. Then sit before your guiding spirit for a few minutes and then mentally take leave and slowly come out of the meditation.

5. Our personal or seminal sound

In each individual there is a seminal (personal and overall) sound. This sound determines our individual characteristics – our temperament, our inclinations, the level of our perception and our personal capacities.

We carry this sound as a vibration in our personal atmosphere. The people we come across can perceive this sound as 'our presence'. It tells them many things about us. They can feel it directly. Hence, people are not easily deceived by the impressions we try to make on them!

People can also know the quality of the sound you carry *indirectly* by observing the way you live and think; from your special interests; and from your personal response to the happenings in your environment.

This seminal sound is instrumental in bringing together people who carry a similar vibration (as in a family). It also draws people to certain kinds of situations in their life. They choose them subconsciously. Thus, their joy or sorrow, their luck or misfortune, and their good or bad companions are not simply granted to them. They are drawn towards them by the vibration they carry.

6. How chanting alters our personal vibration

When we practice chanting regularly, we nurture a spiritual vibration in our system. The chanting changes our vibration (the seminal sound in our personal atmosphere), which in turn changes our inclinations. As a result we begin to think differently, we feel differently and we respond to the happenings in outer life differently. It totally changes our attitude, how we regard things (what arguments we buy into) and where (in what places) we look for our satisfaction.

Hence, the chanting practice not only improves our concentration, but it also builds our character. Then our spiritual task is to simply correct our habitual response and make it more consistent with what we perceive to be true or proper.

7. Should you begin the practice with chanting or meditation (without mantra)?

Meditation calms and refreshes the mind. However, the impurities in the mind remain unaltered in this process. Hence, the changes are not lasting.

The *sensual* attractors like lust, taste and intoxication, sensational music, etc. remain. The attraction to physical beauty and aversion to ugliness remains. The *emotional* attractors like self-esteem issues and craving for importance or attention remains. Suppressed emotions like jealousy, revenge and trauma remains. And the *mental* attractors like personal ambition, greed and intellectual pride remain unaltered.

So what happens? You land up meditating on these things. Then, instead of overcoming the ego and selfish inclinations, the meditation practice makes you more egoistic! On the other hand, the chanting practice reduces the hold that such things have on you by altering your seminal sound. Hence, the process of readjusting your habits and tendencies continues.

Thus, people who follow the way of meditation often get stuck, whereas those who do chanting quickly pass on to the next stage of the practice.

8. Is the practice of meditation in mantra yoga theistic or atheistic?

The meditation practice that is popular in the modern society is *atheistic*. Here we keep the mind idle for a long period of time so that it can become empty of its contents. It will overcome your mental restlessness and give you the experience of a stillness that exists behind the mental activity.

A necessary part of this discipline is to live a very humble life and to reject the sensual cravings. However, this part of the practice is usually overlooked by the people who practice it in the modern world. When that happens, the practice develops many contradictions in the personality. Further, since the connection with the higher consciousness is not established, the practice usually drifts into the psychological dimension like overcoming complexes or into humanitarian pursuits like compassion. It does not unveil the spiritual being.

The *theistic* approach to meditation is quite different. Here we meditate on the image of

God to awaken spiritual qualities in our inner life. The meditation is more like contemplation and it is done for short durations. In this approach you do not have to develop the ability to meditate for long durations to empty the mind. Instead you have to develop the ability to perceive the presence of the higher consciousness. Then you know that there is a spiritual being that is taking care of you. Hence, you can live your life spontaneously and accept the situations of life as they arrive.

c) On controlling Thoughts and Emotions

After you have achieved some control over your attention, you can direct it inward. Then you become aware of the influence exerted by your personal thoughts and emotions in your life. The thoughts are like the seeds of your actions, and your actions have a great influence on the happenings in your life. Hence, by exercising control over the negative thoughts and negative emotions that occupy your mind you can change many things. You can use it to become more peaceful, more understanding and more successful in your undertakings.

1. Dealing with intruding thoughts

There are two ways: *Withdraw* your attention
from a disturbing thought, or *substitute* the
unwanted thought with your favourite (good)
thought.

Example: If a girl doesn't want to go out with
you, what does she do? She looks away and
ignores you. Or she says: *"I've got someone
else".* However, she doesn't argue (entangle)
with you by asking: *"Why should I want to go
with you?"* You can deal with most intruding
thoughts in this way. Just withhold your
attention and refuse to get involved with the
thought: Don't indulge in it, don't elaborate it
and don't argue with it. Then, as an old
acquaintance it can still enter your mind.
However, if it cannot get your attention, it
cannot stay or sustain long enough in your mind.
Then it cannot change the experience in your
mind or influence your thinking and actions.

The practice: To a thought that persistently
intrudes in your mind and distracts you, say:
"Hello there, you again? All right, stay if you

like; go if you like — I'm not going along with you." The thought will try to make you feel that you are *'losing out'* or *'missing out'* or *'being deprived'* of something. However, if you are not deceived by such suggestions and persist in ignoring the thought, it will have to look elsewhere for its feed.

The method of substituting the thought also works well. When you entertain your favourite thought, it will automatically displace the unwanted thought. You can also use the mantra to displace the unwanted thought.

2. Dealing with troublesome thoughts

We think some thoughts, but some thoughts also 'think us'! That is, they can decide to arise in our mind and cause us to think or feel in a particular way. They can overpower our judgement and *compel* us to act according to their dictates. Then we helplessly serve their intentions. Such thoughts are usually associated in our mind with emotions of greed, fear, lust, jealousy and revenge.

A psychic can actually see the thought entities hanging around in our mental atmosphere. From time to time such a thought dips into our mind and feeds on our attention. In this way it continuously distracts our attention to keep its hold on us.

Why are some thoughts able to force their way into our mind? They can do that because we are entangled with them in some way — by our attitudes, beliefs and desires. And that gives them a right to enter. Hence, we cannot outright reject them. However, we can choose to *bind* the thought and restrict its entry in our mind. Then, instead of submitting to the thought unconditionally, we can set some conditions and grant it a limited or conditional access. For example, we can schedule the time or place for its feed — when we shall allow it. Then, at other times we shall find it easier to resist that thought. In this way we can break our slavery to a particular thought or desire.

When we decide to feed the thought at a scheduled time we do admit a partial failure. However, by rejecting the thought at other times we also achieve a *partial victory*! In time such partial victories add up and go to strengthen our will power.

A summary: The thoughts that you think translate into your mind as plans; the plans translate into actions; and the actions translate into events and happenings in your world. Hence, to be 'in charge' of your life, you must be able to exercise your mastery over the thoughts you think. You have to always remain aware of your thoughts and the direction in which they are taking you. Weed out the unwanted thoughts and reinforce the desired thoughts. Just get busy doing this task and very soon you will find that everything will change for the better in your life.

3. How do emotions arise?

An emotion is a vital energy with a quality. Negative emotions arise in the mind due to our personal (egoistic) reaction to a thought or a happening. Normally, emotions follow thoughts. For example: What happens when your expectations are frustrated? *Anger* arises. What happens when you look at people who are more fortunate? *Jealousy* arises. What happens when you experience defeat or do not get what you want? *Sadness* arises. What happens when you attain or accomplish something? *Pride* arises.

4. Dealing with negative emotions

An emotion arises due to our *personal reaction* to a thought or happening. Hence, the key factor in controlling our emotions is to break our habit of interpreting the happenings in life very personally.

What happens when we take things personally? Then our mind becomes open to negative emotions. Then we lose our objectivity; we become psychological and get disturbed.

What is the process? First, our mind registers a fact. Then, the ego comes in to give it a personal interpretation. Hence, our task is to *separate* the fact from our interpretation of it. Then we can keep our objectivity and respond to the situation intelligently. Then we don't become tense, self-righteous and stubborn; we are not easily annoyed, bothered or depressed.

5. Clearing negative emotions

Whenever something happens that generates a strong reaction in you, don't justify the reaction. Then it will lose its force and its hold in you. Then you will be able to *reject* the emotion. To reject the emotion, chant the mantra until the emotion has subsided. Then release the energy. Let go of it.

The rule is that we have to *'mind ourselves'*. We have to learn to manage what goes on inside our mind as a consequence of what has happened in the outer environment! We cannot control the happenings in the outer world, but we can always control what is happening inside our mind as a consequence of what happens outside.

A review Request

Now that you have read the book thus far, could you grant me the favour of writing a review for this book on Amazon?

It will do two things: It will tell other readers what they can realistically expect from reading this book; and it will tell me what you want or value so that I can, in future, produce the kind of books that will benefit my readers the most. *Here are the steps:*

- Click Amazon.com or the Amazon site in your country.
- Sign into Amazon as you are prompted.
- Select an appropriate rating.
- Write a few honest words that describe your impressions in a box.
- Give a heading to the box.
- Click the 'submit' button

It's easy to do and I'll really appreciate it. Click http://www.amazon.com/dp/B0176HQSOG

Thanks.
Prashant

ABOUT THE AUTHOR

He was educated in Chemistry at Massachusetts Institute of Technology (BS), and University of California, (MS & PhC), and initiated into Yoga-Mysticism by Shri Nyaya Sharma — a Master of Shiva-Tantra-Yoga.

He is a counsellor and a spiritual guide. He conducts 'Spiritual Development COURSES' on the internet through Darshana Centre (darshanacentre@gmail.com). He also conducts 'Spiritual Awareness WORKSHOPS' in India, USA and UK. He speaks and writes clearly, in simple language, and from personal experience.

He is the AUTHOR of the books: The Crisis of Modern Humanity (1976); The Essence of Hindu Astrology (1987); The Practice of Mysticism (2009); The Art of Awakening the Soul (2011); Healing without Drugs (2014); The Biochemic Prescriber (2016); and How to Restore your Health Naturally (2017). For details, visit the Site on Internet at http:// spiritual-living.in

OTHER BOOKS & ARTICLES

By the Author

The articles are related to our subject. They are from the blogs on the author's site at http://spiritual-living.in. The three books discussed herein below are available from Amazon (printed) and Kindle bookstore.

1. The Virtue of Slowing Down (Article)
2. The Five Stages of Improvement (Article)
3. Healing without Drugs (Book)
4. Art of Awakening the Soul (Book)
5. The Biochemic Prescriber (Book)
6. How to Restore your Health Naturally (Book)

1. The Virtue of Slowing Down

Quote from a song by Simon & Garfunkel:
"Slow down, you move too fast; you've got to make the moment last; just sitting around and kicking the corner stone; looking for fun and feeling groovy..."

In the modern world people try to get things done fast and play busy. Hence, it is important to see the great virtue of moving slowly and not hurrying through life.

When we are at peace with ourselves, we rarely choose to be in a hurry. Hence, hurrying up is an egoistic movement that pushes us to get things done, as though that is all that matters right now. But when we keep on hurrying, our life becomes superficial. Although we can be satisfied with the results we have for a while, the joy does not last. Soon we become dissatisfied or bored and begin to rush into doing something else. *Let us try to understand why this happens.*

When we rush, we act like an automaton or a machine. Then we are consumed by doing things that can increase the 'quantity', but not the 'quality' of our life. Further, it makes us respond to the ego's wants and not to the deeper wants of our true, inner being. Then, we don't seek the joy from living, but we seek it from getting more money or more power. It can give us some temporary satisfaction, but we have to keep on chasing things to sustain it.

When we slow down our pace of life and combine it with a devotional attitude, we can access a spiritual presence that is itself joyful and filled with wisdom. On the other hand, when we combine hurrying up with personal ambition, we view our life through the lens of fear, scarcity and competition. Then we cannot trust life and allow it to look after us. Instead, we have to cope with our fears and insecurities by constantly pushing ourselves to do something. It gets us caught up in the ego's world, where we can never be at rest or just be. It makes us lose our touch with a spiritual presence which seems to tell us all is going to be well.

If we are truly thoughtful, we can understand that our life is much more than just getting things done; that there has to be something deeper and more mysterious behind all this outer activity that makes sense of the drama of our life. We can intuitively begin to understand that there is a spiritual presence behind the happenings of life; and that it is guiding us to move us naturally and spontaneously in various ways.

However, as long as we keep on hurrying through our activities, we march to the drumbeat of our ego. Then we don't notice what else is there besides the ego's voice in our head; and we don't notice the spiritual presence at the core of our being that is continuously seeking to guide us.

Further, we don't take the time to do the little things that this spiritual presence suggests — like just hanging around peacefully; being patient with other people; playing with animals or children, being present to the situation that you are in; or simply sending off a kind email to a friend. The ego doesn't initiate such acts because it does not perceive any value in them. Such acts are motivated by our spiritual being, and not by our ego.

The strange thing is that when we slow down, we actually find the time to do such little things. We do them because it makes us feel good about doing them. We feel that doing such things is worthwhile. However, if we keep up a fast pace of life, we only amplify the ego's voice that says: *"Hurry up; you still have a lot more to do; you'll never get it done in time; you didn't do that well; you cannot have the time for doing such little things..."*

The voice of the ego not only disconnects us from the 'quiet voice of our higher consciousness', but it also keeps us stressed-out and not feeling too good about ourselves. So, when we find that we have gotten into such a state, all we have to do to regain our perspective is to simply slow down. It will make us look at life through different eyes and feel it with a different heart. Then, instead of being lost in the ego's ideas about what our life should look like, we can accept life as it is and as it comes. It will make our life more joyful, meaningful and valuable to us and to others.

2. The Five Stages of Improvement

An Autobiography

Chapter-1:

I took a walk in the street.

There was a large pothole.

I didn't notice it in time, so I fell in.

Then I started to blame others.

I was upset, so I took time to come out.

Chapter-2:

I took a walk in the same street.

There was a large pothole.

I noticed it, but I didn't act in time, so I fell in again.

I knew I shouldn't have fallen in, but I still preferred to blame others.

I was upset, so I took time to come out.

Chapter-3:

I again took a walk in the same street.

The large pothole was still there.

This time I tried to walk around it, but still I fell in — it has become a habit.

I knew I shouldn't have fallen in, so this time I accepted it as my fault.

I wasn't upset, so I could get out quickly.

Chapter-4:

I still took a walk in the same street.

The large pothole was still there.

I was careful, so I could walk around it without falling in.

Chapter-5:

Now I take my walk in a different street.

There is no pothole.

Some Interesting Observations:

The narration of the five stages of improvement is SYMBOLIC. Read the observations by our readers:

By Ginger M:

What is so interesting about this *'autobiography'*? It's like a whack on the side of our head. It shows us what commonly happens as we try to improve ourselves! Our habits are rooted in the subconscious, and hence we are not sufficiently aware of how we act. We fall many times before we get things right.

By Frank Sanchez

The chapters of this "Autobiography" are small, but they reveal a great truth. Here are my observations:

1. We can't avoid what we don't see. That is the beginner's position. Hence, we blame other people for our misfortunes and don't initiate any changes.

2. As we use our experience, we acknowledge our contribution to the making of our troubles. But still have to take the necessary action. Mere knowing does not change the reality. Hence, we keep on getting the same old results.

3. In the next step we begin to make the necessary changes. However, we are so accustomed to doing things in our old ways that our pattern repeats. At this stage we know the real reason for our failure. Hence, we don't blame others. We know what we have to do to overcome our problem.

4. Now we see the problem and we are able to overcome it.

5. Ultimately we become farsighted. Then we can easily avoid the problem.

By Madanda Machayya:

I explain this line by line. Note, the 1st line shows our habit; the 2nd line shows the problem that awaits us in the outer world; the 3rd line shows what usually happens as we try to change the habit; the 4th line speaks of our reaction or the self-assessment that happens as we make improvements; and the 5th line explains the extra difficulties we create for ourselves.

3. Healing Without Drugs

A Simple Solution to your Health Problems

152 pages; ISBN-13: 978-145242793; ISBN-10:
149524279X; ASIN: BOOHYR3RRA. The URL is
http://www.amazon.com/dp/BOOHYR3RRA

The Message:

Your health is always your concern and not your doctor's concern. However, today the people are made to believe that their health depends on doctors and the healthcare system! It has made the people unnecessarily dependent on the medical profession. On the other side the healthcare system has become extremely expensive, and the issues of health have become too technical and complicated for the common man to comprehend.

However, this should not dishearten you since you can learn to maintain your health with your own efforts. All you have to do is to think holistically and take the simple self-help measures that can restore your health and keep you healthy. The know-how on how you can do it is adequately provided in this book.

The Methods:

You use simple methods like good eating habits, elimination diets, water therapy, fasting, etc. to bring about lasting relief to many of your long standing problems. In this way you not only restore your health, but you also build your immunity to disease.

The book also talks about psychosomatic causes of diseases and how to deal with them. In particular, you learn to deal with the issues of stress, trauma, karmic causes, and how to benefit from pranic healing.

An Estimate:

Holistic healing is not something that is done to you. You have consciously or unconsciously participated in generating the causes of your ailment. Hence, you have to also participate in overcoming the cause. You have to make the necessary adjustments in your mindset, eating habits and emotions to overcome the cause of your ailments.

An Overview of the Chapters

- The 'Forward' and 'Preface' tell you the point of view adopted in this book.
- Chapter-1 discusses the basic concept of holistic healing.

- Chapter-2 explains the rationale of naturopathy.
- Chapter-3 discusses the most convenient and effective remedies for self-healing.
- Chapter-4 explores the deeper causes, like stress, trauma and karma, which underlie the basic disease factor of Toxaemia in the body.
- Chapter-5 discusses the theory and practice of pranic healing, which is exceptionally useful in healing deeper organ troubles, backaches, psychosomatic disorders and psychological troubles.

4. The Art of Awakening the Soul

Practical Yoga-Mysticism

143 pages, ISBN-13: 978-1460906033, ISBN-10: 1460906039, ASIN: BOOAX19BRW; URL is http://www.amazon.com/dp/B00AXI9BRW/

In this book you learn the practical art of attuning your mind with a higher consciousness. Then instead of being guided by the tendencies in your mind, you will be guided by a higher consciousness

This practice will gradually bring the soul forward in your life. The soul is your inner companion and it will give you the experience of deep love that cannot be got through the people and things of the outer world.

When the soul is sufficiently awake in your life, it will guide you, inform you, and make you intuitive. Then everything in your life will begin to fall into its proper place: You will know what to do with your life and your time; you will get the opportunities you really need; and the rest will not matter very much.

The Contents:

1. Foreword by the Author
2. What is Mysticism?
3. The Practice

5. The Biochemic Prescriber

A handy guide for prescribing Dr. Schuessler's biochemic tissue salts to family and friends

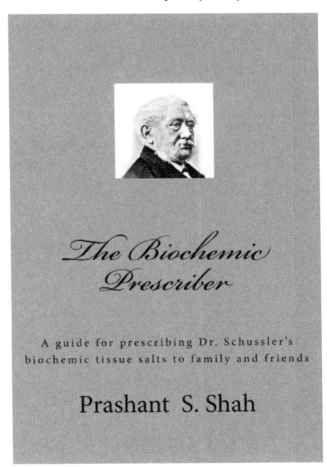

The Biochemic Prescriber

A guide for prescribing Dr. Schussler's biochemic tissue salts to family and friends

Prashant S. Shah

Biochemic medicine was discovered over a hundred years ago by a German physician, Dr. Wilhelm Heinrich Schuessler. He identified twelve inorganic tissue-salts that are essential for the healthy functioning of the human body. He showed that when there is a deficiency of any of these salts in the body tissues, certain typical symptoms arise. You can use these symptoms *to identify* the specific deficiency.

Then all you have to do is supplement the deficient tissue-salt in a dynamic (potency 6X) form. That will stimulate the vital force to become active and do the healing.

This system is simple to understand and easy to use. And it comes without the 'side-effects' that usually arise from using the drug therapy. The most interesting thing about this approach to healing is that you don't need to know in detail the functions of the body organs or the classification of disease; and you don't have to rely on all kinds of laboratory tests to be able to prescribe.

Here is an up-to-date, clear, and concise book that you can use to heal yourself, your family and friends. It tells you how you can treat the common everyday ailments that arise. The book is simple to understand and easy to use; and the results are very consistent and satisfying.

The Contents

1. Some Reviews
2. Author's Preface
3. A Synopsis
4. Introduction
5. The Guiding Symptoms
6. On using the guiding symptoms
7. The Prescription
8. Case taking:
9. Repetitions:
10. Do 'side-effects' arise from using these tissue salts?
11. Why are there no biochemic practitioners?
12. On Readymade Formulations
13. Leading Remedies for Common Diseases

The book is available from
Kindle online store:
https://www.amazon.com/dp/B01FA6X4FG/
Amazon online store:
http://www.amazon.com/dp/1533128065

6. How to Restore your Health Naturally

A time-tested way to heal yourself by simply changing your lifestyle and eating habits

ISBN-13: 978-1977555472; ISBN-10: 1977555470. The URL is https://www.amazon.in/dp/B075V5R1FJ

Today we are ingrained to believe that our health depends on doctors, medicines, and the health care industry; whereas the truth is that our health really depends on our lifestyle, diet and emotions. When we understand this simple truth, we can learn to restore and maintain our health by our own efforts and, except in extreme cases, we will not need to consult doctors.

The method of natural healing that we show is holistic and totally different from the specialised advice that you normally receive through the medical profession. It is simple, and to use it you do not need to know anatomy, physiology, pathology, toxicology or pharmacology. Further, the results of this treatment are self-evident, and so you do not have to depend on empirical proofs.

You simply learn to strengthen the vital force in the body and help it in its effort to restore your health and keep you healthy.

Contents:

1. Foreword

2. Introduction
3. The medical profession focuses on relieving symptoms
4. What is so wrong with just relieving symptoms?
5. The holistic and analytic approaches to healing
6. Understanding disease in terms of toxaemia and the vital force
7. Aren't germs and bacteria the causes of disease?
8. How to detoxify the body
9. Reduce the existing toxaemia
10. Avoid generating toxins
11. Correct your eating habits
12. On emotional causes
13. What causes the vital force to become weak?
14. The elimination crisis
15. If natural healing is so simple, why isn't everyone doing it?
16. Our message

Printed in Great Britain
by Amazon

79095961R00078